First Edition
(1998/1418)

MUSLIMS IN AMERICA

Seven Centuries of History

(1312-1998)

Collections and Stories of American Muslims

Amir Nashid Ali Muhammad

amana publications
Beltsville, MD

297.0973
M952

amana publications
10710 Tucker Street
Beltsville, Maryland 20705-2223 USA
Tel: (301)595-5777 Fax: (301)595-5888
E-mail: igamana@erols.com
Website: www.amana-publications.com

Library of Congress Catalogue-in-Publication Data
Muhammad, Amir N. (Amir Nashid)
    Muslims in America : seven centuries of history,
1312-1998 : collections and stories of American
Muslims / Amir N. Muhammad.
        p.   cm.
    ISBN 0-915957-78-7
    1. Islam--United States--History.   2. Muslims--United
States--History.   3. Black Muslims--United States--
History.   4. Afro-Americans--Religion.   I. Title.
BP67.U6M8 1998
297'.0973--dc21   97-52570
                                                              CIP

Printed in the United States of America by
International Graphics
10710 Tucker Street
Beltsville, Maryland 20705-2223 USA
Tel: (301) 595-5999 Fax: (301) 595-5888
E-mail: igfx@aol.com

CONTENTS

Maps and Pictures

Foreword

A merican Muslims are now a part of the cultural land-
scape of the United States of America. Their num-
bers have grown significantly over the last four decades.
Because of this growing visibility and self-confidence,
many of them with the ability to do research have begun
to publish works designed to increase the knowledge of
the average American about the history and development of Islam in the United States. As a result, a growing
body of literature on American Muslims is developing
throughout the country. The publication in your hand is
one of the latest in the expanding number of printed
works seeking a respectable place in the library of the
reading American public.

The material presented within this book is the fruit of
many hours of tedious research in libraries and other
places where researchers could secure materials that can
shed light on the young Muslim community and in the
United States. Mr. Muhammad has spent time talking to
a variety of Muslims about this project and his work
should be seen as one of the pioneering efforts to fill
gaps in the historical record of our community. As a
brick in the edifice of American Muslim scholarship, this
work is recommended to Muslims and non-Muslims who
are genuinely interested in knowing how Muslims came
to the U.S. and what the major historical events are that
identify the birth and development of this community of
believers.

The work does not claim to be exhaustive; however, one can say that its contribution will be judged not only for the dates it provides but also for the chronology of events that give significance and meaning to Muslim life and history on this continent. Those who take time to go over it will walk away enriched by its contents.

Sulayman S. Nyang, Ph.D.
Professor of African Studies
Howard University

Letter from the Director of Collections and Stories of American Muslims (CSAM)

Bismi-llah
(In the Name of God)

When my husband told me he was going to write a book about American Muslims, highlighting the experiences of slaves who were Muslims, I was overwhelmed and didn't quite feel his passion; I had already read many books written about Muslims and Muslim slaves. However, with his perseverance, constant researching, re-editing, rewriting, and probing, it became evident that his work would be a very special and inclusive historical text. You can definitely feel his passion in this book.

As this is the first edition, I know that in time more historical facts will be added, more research will be done to further enhance it. Books are constantly being written by scholars around the world and Amir has proven himself to be a scholar in his own right. I am certain his book will be given the recognition it deserves. Amir's work will encourage you to want to know more about Muslims living in America

As Collections and Stories of American Muslims (traveling exhibition and archives) emerges as a forthright cultural and historical institution, *Muslims in America: Seven Centuries of History* (1312–1997) sets the proper tone for our endeavors. Amir's book is an important step toward the further understanding of and appreciation for the Islamic history of Muslims in America. May Allah bless Amir for his efforts and endeavors.

Habeebah D. Muhammad
Director, CSAM

Message from the President of CSAM

M*uslims in America: Seven Centuries of History* was published to help educate the American society, as well as the global community about Islam's history and contributions in America. This collection of stories and history is the first step toward creating a museum for Muslim Americans.

In it, we will find many fascinating stories and insightful historical events. The story of Job Ibn Solomon Jallo will remind us of the Quranic and Biblical stories of the Prophet Job's life and struggles. This book will make any American Muslim proud to know that there were some Muslims who, in the War of 1812, helped defend the country against the British.

When we read the story of Bilali Muhammad (Ben Ali), we are inspired by the Islamic community he helped build in Georgia while he was a slave. We see his determined to hold on to his Islamic life, no matter what his condition and circumstances. In some ways his life parallels the life of Bilal Ibn Rabah, a companion of the Prophet Muhammad (peace and blessing be upon him), who was a slave in Makkah at the time of the Prophet Muhammad. His strength and courage exercised for the sake of his deen (religion) can be held up as a model.

Collections and Stories of American Muslims. (CSAM) was created in 1996 to establish an Islamic traveling exhibition in America and abroad. The exhibit will reflect America's Islamic history and culture.

CSAM is seeking contributions, information, materials, artifacts, and stories to enhance and progress the development of its project.

If you have or are aware of any information that can assist in this endeavor, please contact us at:

Collections and Stories of American Muslims
2524 Elvans Road
Washington, D.C. 20020
(202) 678-6906
E-mail amir@amermuslim.org

Introduction

Bismi-llah
(In the name of Allah)

Subhanahu Wa Ta'ala
(May God be praised and may
His transcendence be affirmed)

And hold firm to the rope of Allah together and do not separate yourselves. (Quran 3:103)

A gainst extreme odds, Islam has discretely survived in the fiber of the American society. In the New World, some of the African slaves suffered a doubly tragic fate. Initially, they were enslaved because they were African, but when it was discovered that they were also Muslims, their suffering was compounded. They were tortured, burned alive, hung, and shot unless they renounced their religion and their names. At least 20% of the Africans brought to the U.S. were Muslims from empires governed by Islam. Documented cases of enslaved African Muslims show that they originally came from the coastal and interior regions of the Islamic empires of Songhai, Ghana, and Mali.

The early Muslim community in the U.S. should be remembered for their strong devotion to Islam under such awful conditions. The social life and language of the direct descendants of the first Muslim community helped form the inspiration of the African American Muslims known as the Gullah* people, whose language and culture helped facilitate communications among the various tribes. Some common words used in the South, such as goober (peanut), gumbo (okra), ninny (female breast), tote (to carry), and yam (sweet potato); and names like Bobo (one who cannot talk), Geeji (a language and tribe in Liberia), Agona (a country in Ghana), Ola (that which saves), Samba (a Hausa name given to the second son), and Zola (to love). came from the influence of these people. The Muslims also have contributed many Arabic words found in English, such as admiral, algebra, amber, atlas, banana, cable, camel, checkmate, coffee, cotton, jasmine, lemon, magazine, mask, musk, rice, sofa, sugar, syrup, and zero to name a few.

In addition, in the 1960s Muslims, particularly those from the Nation of Islam, had a tremendous impact on the consciousness of Black movements.

During the 1970s, Muslims and Islam influenced America's music culture with the message songs of the

---

* The Gullah, or Geechee are a group of African Americans who came from different ethnic groups of West Africa. The Gullah people have been able to retain more of their African heritage than other African Americans. They spoke a similar language and shared similar crafts, foods, music, folk tales, architecture, textiles, and belief systems in South Carolina and coastal Georgia.

Philadelphia Sound. The Muslim influence of the people's champion, Muhammad Ali, ignited pride and dignity within the Black community. The Islamic life of Kunte Kinte, portrayed in Alex Haley's book *Roots (The Saga of an American Family)*, motivated many Americans to research their family's history.

In the 1980s, Islam once again influenced the cultural identity of African Americans when they became known as African Americans instead of Black Americans.

I pray that you will enjoy and be enriched by America's Islamic history contained in the pages that follow. As more information comes to us we will, *insha' Allah* (God willing), continue to publish and evolve the Collections and Stories of American Muslims' Museum.

I thank Allah (God) for His blessings and mercy, and for my parent's Herbert and Mabel West for their love. I would like to express my appreciation to Allah for revealing to me, through my father's blood line, my direct, seventh generation ancestor from Africa, Clara Higginbotham. Clara was born in West Africa in 1793. She was enslaved sometime in the early 1800s in Brunswick, Georgia.

In 1870 one of Clara's daughters, Amry Bakr, was living with her. Because Bakr (now Baker) is a very familiar name among Muslims, I became curious and after some research found that Salih Bilali, one of the enslaved Muslims highlighted in this book, lived less than 15 miles away from Clara on St. Simons, during this period of time.

Through my genealogical research and after having discovered my African ancestry, I was driven to study the history of Islam in America. Lastly, I would like to thank my wife Habeebah Muhammad, and the staff of the AMC (American Muslim Council)—Fahhim Abdulhadi, Hanan Williams, and Suraiya Hassan—for the time and energy they spent editing this book.

Amir N. Muhammad
Author and Researcher

EARLY HISTORY

Historical Moments

In 1312, African Muslims arrived in the Gulf of Mexico for exploration of the American interior using the Mississippi River as their access route. These Muslim explorers were from Mali and other parts of West Africa. The brother of Mansa Musa, Abubakari, was one of the first to set sail to America from Africa.

In 1492, when Christopher Columbus arrived in the New World, he was strongly influenced by the geography of the 13th-century Arab scholar, Al-Idrissi, who served as an adviser to King Roger of Sicily. Columbus had with him a copy of Al-Idrissi's works mentioning the discovery of a new continent by eight Muslim explorers. He also had some Muslim crew members with him for translation and other services.

In 1527, Estevanico of Azamor, a Muslim from Morocco, arrived in Florida with the ill-fated expedition of Panfilo de Narvaez.

In 1539, Estevanico was one of the first of three Americans to cross this continent. At least two states, Arizona and New Mexico, owe their beginning to his explorations.

THE 1700s

Historical Moments

In 1713, the practice of polygamy among Muslim slaves in New England and New York was reported by the Reverend John Sharpe of New York. He explained that there were what he called "negro marriages" without the consent of the church. Some slaves, he went on to say, were practicing polygamy and none of the wives were willing to accept a divorce.

In 1719, in Milton, Massachusetts, Reverend Peter Thatcher wrote about a Muslim woman named Hagar who had three children—Sambo, Jimmie, and Hagar—and whose husband, also named Sambo, disappeared in 1719.

In 1753, two men, Abel Conder and Mahamut, petitioned the South Carolina royal authorities in Arabic; they were Moors from Sali on the Barbary Coast of Africa. Around 1736, a battle was lost with the Portuguese and they were captured. An officer, Captain Henry Daubrib, asked the Moors if they were willing to serve him for five years in Carolina, they agreed. When they arrived in South Carolina they were transferred to Daniel LaRoche, who then enslaved them for fifteen years until they petitioned the authorities for their freedom.

In 1777, under the leadership of Mohammed III, Morocco was the first country in the world to recognize the independence of the United States and granted free rights of passage to all American ships.

In 1786, two men appeared in Charleston, SC dressed like Moors. They had aroused a great deal of suspicion by their strange attire and ways, resulting in gaining the attention of the law. An officer attempted to question them and found out they were Moors who did not speak English. They were then taken to a lady (on East Bay Street) named Starr Barrett. Starr being Jewish born in the Barbary States spoke and understood Arabic well. She was able to learn that the two men were Algerians who had sailed from Algeria to Virginia where they had been arrested. They then traveled overland to South Carolina.

In 1787 on the Delaware River, the Treaty of Peace and Friendship was signed between the United States and Morocco bearing the signatures of Abdel-Khak, Muhammad Ibn Abdullah, and George Washington.

In 1790, South Carolina passed the Moors Sundry Act which was enacted by the legislative body to grant special status to the subjects of the sultan of Morocco. Free Moors by the names of Francis, Daniel, Hammond, and Samuel, along with their wives Fatima, Flora, Sarah, and Clarinda asked the South Carolina House of Representatives to treat them as free whites. They petitioned the legislature to rule that they were not subject to the laws that governed blacks and slaves.

8

In **1790** in South Carolina, the Sumter county census recorded the name of Joseph Benenhaly. Actually, his name was Yusef Ben Ali and he was a Muslim from Morocco. It is recorded that Yusef Benenhaly was recruited by General Thomas Sumter to fight with him in the American Revolution. After the war, Sumter took him inland to Stateburg where he settled down and where many of his descendants remain today. His dark-skinned descendants are known as the "Turks of Sumter County." The Turks claimed the lands along the southern coast of the Mediterranean as a part of their empire.

Special note: The African-born Muslim named Quosh (Quash) Freeman of Derby, Connecticut was well known for his strength and size. He was a slave of Agar Tomlinson, a prominent and wealthy man of New England.

There are many reports of African slaves with Muslim names in New England like, Hamet, a noted craftsman of toy drums living in Middletown, Connecticut; and Occramer Marycoo, whose musical talent was well known in Newport, Rhode Island.

The Slavery Years

It is recorded that between 15 and 30 percent of Africans brought to North America between 1731 and 1867 were Muslims. During the slave trading years, more than 10 million Africans were taken from their lands.

About fifty African Muslim slaves are well known by name and reference. The word Mandinga means "book man" (a reflection of Muslim literacy). However, not all

Muslims were Mandingas and not all Mandingans were Muslim.

Many African Muslims came to America from south of the Sahara desert between Senegal and Lake Chad. They were Fula, Fulbe, Fulani, Hausa, Manding, Mandinga, Massina, Kanuri, Kassonke, Serahule, Temne, Mende, Moor, and Arab.

They were of the Islamic empires of Songhai, Ghana, and Mali, and came from places like Timbo, Futa Jallon (present day Guinea), Conakry, Ghana, Congo, Angola, Senegambia, Sierra Leone, Nigeria, and Bundu (the eastern region of present day Senegal).

During the 1730s, there were among the Muslims taken into slavery at least three who became well known, Job ibn Solomon, Yarrow Mamout, and Lamine Jay. Later in the century, there was Ibrahim Abdul Rahahman (known as the prince of slaves) and Mohamet a well known runaway slave from around Savannah, Georgia.

Later in the 1700s and the 1800s came Kunta Kinte, Lamen Kebe, Omar ibn Said, Salih Bilali, Samba, Bilali (known as Ben Ali and Abu Ali), Charno, Osman, Abu Bakr, Mohammed Kaba, Mohammed, and Abu Muhammad Abdullah ibn abi Zaid al-Qairawani, to name a few.

Some came from prominent and powerful families. They were teachers, cavalry leaders, religious leaders, and students of law. There are at least 8 known Muslim slaves who ran away from their slave masters—3 were captured again and 5 escaped. Some were able to win their freedom and return to Africa, while others were able to become trusted slave managers.

Job ibn Solomon Jallo

Job ibn Solomon Jallo was a trader and religious leader (Imam) who came from Bundu, Senegal. He was captured in the Gambia in 1730 and brought to Annapolis, Maryland, where he was purchased in 1731. Job was a slave for about two years in Maryland after which he was taken to England and set free. He returned to his home in 1734, as a Royal African Company representative. Job's name in Africa was Ayuba ibn Solomon ibn Ibrahim Jallo (Job son of Solomon son of Abraham Jallo).

From *Gentlemen's Magazine* (1750).

Job was the son of an *imam* (leader of the prayer) in Bundu. Reports describe him as a well-mannered, courtly, intelligent, monotheistic, and literate human being who came out of Africa. As a slave he was allowed a place to pray and other conveniences in order to make his slavery as easy as possible. Job was a *hafiz,** who wrote out by hand three copies of the Quran from memory. He was married to two wives before his capture. His first wife was the daughter of the *alpha*** of Tombut and together they had three children Abdullah, Samba, and Ibrahim. Job's second wife was the daughter of the *alpha* of Tomga together they had a daughter named Fatima.

---

* A hafiz is someone who has memorized the entire Qur'an.

** Alpha is a religious leader (imam)

Job was blessed with winning his freedom and returning home to his family. When he returned home, his entire family was still alive and well. Job's life contains many beautiful stories indicating God's blessings and mercy; it contains the story of how a father's love for his son helped to win the father's freedom.

Others

Lamine Jay came from Futa-Toro, Senegal; he was captured with Job in 1730. They were kidnaped by Mandingoes while trading on the lower Gambia and brought to Annapolis, Maryland. He was known as a linguist (a translator). Jay was returned to Africa in less than five years because of his friend Job's intelligence, personal dignity, and religious piety.

Kunta Kinte was born in 1750, in the village of Juffure in Gambia. In 1767 at the age of 16, Kunta was captured and enslaved. He was shipped to Annapolis, Maryland, on the Lord Ligonier and sold to a Virginia planter. Kunta Kinte fought hard to hold on to his Islamic heritage. He is the great-great-great-great-great grandfather of the world renown writer of *Roots*, Alex Haley.

Muslim Runaways

In 1749 the *Annapolis Maryland Gazette* advertises two runaway slaves, one named "Prince," age 25 from Cambridge in Dorchester County and another named Cuffee. Both were of a yellowish complexion and both ran away from James Wardrop of Upper Malboro, Maryland.

Some of the Muslim runaways were women. One of the first written records of Muslim women was in the *Savannah Georgia Gazette* on November 22, 1769. The paper advertised that six slaves ran away from the M'Gillivray's plantation at Vale-Royal, Georgia. They had just arrived in the county. The women were all from Guinea; their names were Jamina, a stout woman about 20 years old; Belinda 18 years old; and Hagar around 18 years old. The men were all around 23 years of age: Jacob and Charles from Guinea, and Tony who came from Kishee.

One of the first records of Muslims born in America, comes from the *Savannah Georgia Gazette. On* May 11, 1774 an article was printed about two escaped Muslims name Ishmael and Cuffe. Ishmael, who was around twenty-six, was called "Mun." Cuffe, the other man, was around twenty-three years old. The paper reports that "they were known to be born in the county and well set, tolerable, well made, and sensible. They were runaways from the plantation of the late Benjamin Fox at Little-Ogechee, Georgia."

Mahomet (Muhammad), with documents dating back to 1774, was one of the earliest recorded Muslims in Georgia. Mahomet escaped from John Graham's plantation on Augustin's Creek near Savannah, Georgia. On September 7, 1774, his freedom was documented by the *Savannah Georgia Gazette* in an advertisement seeking his capture for more than three years. He was last seen at a settlement near the Indian line on Ogechee.

13

On May 24, 1775, two ads appeared in the *Savannah Georgia Gazette* reporting runaway slaves. The first ad was from the plantation of Lachlan M'Gillivray at Vale-Royal naming three Muslims: Quamie, about 30 years old; Sambo, about 22 years old and a Moor; and another Sambo, about 25 year's old. The second ad came from the plantation of Philip Dell for another slave named Sambo, about 30 years old and born in this country.

In 1787 the *Baltimore Advertiser* and the *Baltimore Maryland Journal* advertised two Muslim runaways; one named Mingo of a yellowish complexion from Baltimore County and another named Anthony a dark mulatto around 23 years old from Talbot County. The ad read "they have the appearance of an Indian or Moor."

In April 1789, an advertisement seeking the capture of a man named Armer (*Amir*) appeared in the *Savannah Georgia Gazette*. Armer was about twenty years old when he ran away from the plantation of Thomas Grave in Richmond County, Georgia.

Osman was a runaway slave who was met by an artist in Virginia. There is not much known about him. On March 18, 1790, the *Savannah Georgia Gazette* advertises two runaway's named Osman and Charles, both of a yellow complexion, tall and slim, and around 26 years old from around Dublin, Great Ogechee, Georgia. Osman was known as the leader of the Dismal Swamp Maroon Community from 1852 to 1862. Osman's leadership proved useful when he made a military alliance with the United States government against the Confederate States of America during the 1860s.

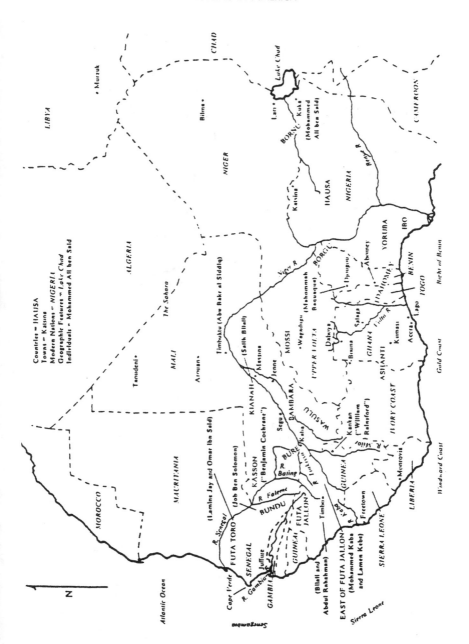

Map I: The Homeland of Captured Muslims

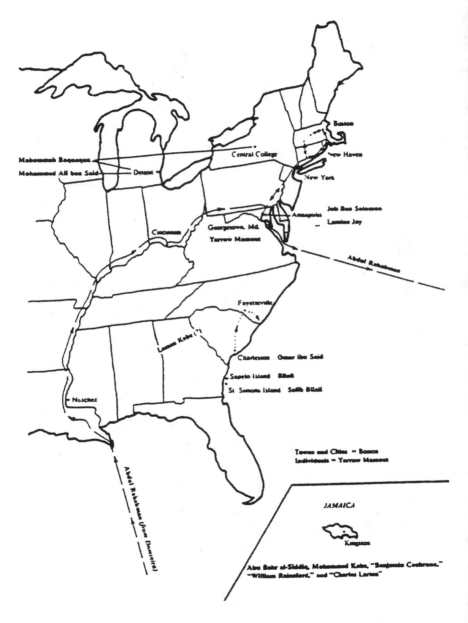

Map II: Known American Homes and Travels

There are many Muslim runaways recorded between 1765 and 1776 with some ads saying yellow complexion and Moorish breed; others giving the names "Moco Prince," "Prince," "Quixote" (Kee), "London," "Africa," "Mingo," "Quamina," to name a few. Also a woman named Hagar is mentioned.

Muslims in America's Early Battles

In 1775 at the Battle of Bunker Hill, Peter Salem's bravery was well noted. He was a slave in Framingham, Massachusetts, shortly before the war. Peter Salem (Saleem) and Salem (Saleem) Poor both fought in the battle and stood out for their extraordinary feats of heroism. It is recorded that Peter Salem won the admiration of his comrades by shooting the British major, Pitcairn, while he was mounting and shouting "the day is ours."

In 1812, during the War with the British, two Muslim slave leaders, both from Georgia's Sea Islands of Sapelo and St. Simon's were armed and prepared to go to war with the British. Both were named Bilali. In 1813, the first warned the British that he had 80 men armed with muskets. Bilali told his master that, in the event of an attack, "I will answer for every Negro of the true faith and not for the Christians you own." On the other hand, Salih Bilali and his master, John Couper lost half of their slave force from St. Simon's Island to the British.

In the Civil War at least two Muslims are known to have fought in the War, Mohammad Ali ibn Said, and Ishmael Hall.

Muslim Involvement in Repatriation

Paul Cuffe was a noted shipbuilder, captain, philanthropist, and nationalist; he was also a descendant of a Muslim family from Ghana. Paul Cuffe was born in 1759 in Cuttyhunk, Massachusetts. His father's name was Saiz Kofi. Paul circumnavigated Africa 18 times and in 1815 he took 38 African-Americans back to freedom to Sierra Leone on his ship. Paul Cuffe was the first black to petition the ruling powers of government to free every slave and to allow every colored man desiring to leave America the freedom to do so.

The 1800s

In the Early 1800s

An 1819 painting of Yarrow Mamout by Charles Peale.

Yarrow Mamout had worked out his freedom and became a landowner and a local character in Georgetown, Washington, DC. He is known to have practiced Islam publicly. By 1807 he was free and had purchased stock in the Columbia Bank, being one of the first to do so.

Yarrow lived to be more than 125 years old. Yarrow's ancestors were from the Shepherd Kings of Egypt. There are two paintings of him today. One hangs in the Historical Society of Pennsylvania and the other at the Georgetown Public Library, Washington, DC.

Lamen Kebe arrived in America early in the 1800s. He was from an elite and sophisticated class of Africans who were trained to rule, advise, teach, protect, trade, translate, go to war, collect taxes, and travel. Kebe was captured in battle. He wrote and read Arabic, and prayed to Allah on the Christian slave ship. Kebe came from

Senegambia, from a famous Serahule family of teachers. They were the founders of ancient Ghana, and they were among the earliest converts to Islam south of the Sahara. His mother was a Mandinga.

Kebe decided against bringing children into the world by forced conception. In slavery he was known as "Old Paul," he learned in three different southern states how ignorant Americans were of Africa. Kebe was freed by 1835 after having been in servitude in South Carolina and Alabama. He returned to Africa at the age of sixty. During the year 1835, Kebe and Omar ibn Sayyid corresponded with each other in Arabic. Kebe, through Omar, provided Theodore Dwight (a member of the American Ethnological Society) with information of his native land, the school system there, and how widespread education was among his people. He also named 30 books written by his people.

Ibrahim Abdul Rahaman

Ibrahim Abdul Rahaman was a calvary leader, who was captured returning home from a successful battle. His homeland was Timbo, (Futa-Jallon) in present day Guinea.

He was a Fulbe (Fulani) and lived from 1762 to 1829. Rahaman had been a student in Timbuktu and still wrote

An engraving of crayon drawing by Henry Inman 1828. From the *Colonizationist and Journal of Freedom* (1834).

22

Arabic after being away for more than thirty years. Rahaman had run away for a little while, but returned to his slave master.

Abdul Rahaman was seen regularly saying his five daily prayers. Once a leader of soldiers in Africa, he became a slave manager in the Natchez area of Mississippi. During the years 1800 to 1818, Rahaman was the sole plantation manager.

He impressed blacks and whites from Cincinnati to Boston to Washington, DC with his dignity and piety. He wrote several short articles and letters for various dignitaries in the United States. One of his letters to Morocco became instrumental in gaining his freedom.

In 1828, at the age of 66, after 40 years of slavery, he finally gained his freedom. After obtaining his freedom he worked to raise money to buy his children's freedom. He and his wife did manage to get to Liberia, but he died before returning to his actual homeland. About a year later eight of his family members were able to join his wife in Liberia using the funds he had raised. Ibrahim Abdul Rahaman was known as the "Prince of Slaves."

Omar ibn (Said) Sayyid

Omar ibn (Said) Sayyid (1770–1864), was a Foula. He was taken from a famous Serahule family of teachers from Fut Tur in present day Senegal.

In his native land before his capture, Omar was married and had a son. He had taught and studied in Bundu.

Omar was a descendant of Arab Muslims who migrated to West Africa in the in the seventh century. Omar was known as a teacher and saint to a few early ethnologists and African colonizationists.

Arriving in America as a slave in 1807, he was shipped to Charleston, South Carolina where he labored for a short time. In 1810, he escaped to North Carolina.

A daguerreotype picture found in the library of Davidson University.

Omar was caught and imprisoned in Fayetteville, North Carolina where he persuaded James Owen, a general in the state militia and brother of John Owen (who later became governor of North Carolina), to purchase him, which he did for $900. He was placed on the Owen Hill plantation where he became a "pampered" slave after convincing his new master that he had a weak constitution.

Omar lived more than a half a century as a storyteller and an oriental (Muslim) saint to neighbors and visitors from near and far. Omar ibn (Said) Sayyid was called "Moreau in slavery." In 1835, Omar wrote a letter to Lahmen (Paul) Kebe, another Muslim slave. In 1836 Paul gave the letter to Theodore Dwight which contained Omar's autobiography. Omar left several short pieces of his writing, which were prayers from the Bible and the Qur'an. Omar's friend, Kebe, wrote him back at least once. After thirty years of being enslaved and away from

24

his homeland, Omar was still able to write Arabic. For some time he prayed, as required of a Muslim, but he found it polite to pretend to be a Christian at times.

Omar did not have any children after he was enslaved. He died in 1864 at the age of 94, and was buried on the Owen Hill plantation in the family burial ground.

A look-alike engraving by James Prichard, in *Researches into the Physical History of Mankind II* (1851).

Salih Bilali

Salih Bilali came from an aristocratic and powerful family of Massina. He was born around 1765. His parents were mixed Mandingan-Fulbe from a town called Kianah in the district of Temourah, along the middle of Niger southwest of Timbuktu. He had learned to read Arabic in Africa. Salih was kidnaped by non-Muslims around 1790 when the Segu Bambara empire was on the rise.

He was only 25 years old when he was kidnaped by the Bambaras north of Jenne along the Niger. They were loaded down with trading items and were forced to march north to the port of Anomabu in present day Ghana. He was taken to the Bahamas and then, in 1800, sold to John Couper.

25

Salih Bilali arrived at St. Simon's, Georgia in 1800 with a friend named Ben Ali (see Bilali Muhammad below). By 1816, Salih Bilali became a trusted head slave manager. He was married to several wives who gave Muslim names and traditions to their American offspring and whose names were recalled as late as the 1930s. Salih created a Muslim community on Georgia's Sea Island of St. Simon. He became locally famous for his efforts during the War of 1812.

Salih was known to have his own Quran and practiced public prayer according to the Quranic obligation despite ridicule and other public pressures. When he lived in Georgia, he was called Tom. Salih had belonged to John Couper and then to his son Hamilton Couper.

He was their trusted head driver for as many as 450 slaves from 1816 to 1846. His master's son proclaimed, while on his death bed, Salih's last words were, "Allah is God and Mohammed his Prophet."

Robert Abbott, a descendant of Salih Bilali, founded the *Chicago Defender,* the nation's first black newspaper. He erected an obelisk in honor of his father and two aunts on the grounds of Fort Frederica on St. Simons Island, Georgia.

Bilali Muhammad

Bilali Muhammad, sometimes called Bu (Abu) Ali, or Ben Ali was a Fula from Timbo Futa Jallon in the highlands of present day Guinea-Conakry. Thomas Spalding of Sapelo

Island, Georgia, brought Bilali and his family as slaves from the Bahamas around 1803. Bilali left a manuscript in Arabic that indicated he was a man trained well beyond the basic Quranic education. His manuscript contained excerpts from a well-known West African legal text of the Maliki school of thought which is predominant in West Africa (i.e., from Morocco to the Gulf of Guinea). The book contained 13 chapters; there were chapters dealing with ablution, the call to prayer, identification with Islamic Law, the Prophet's companions (the *khalifa rashidun:* the four righteous caliphs), and living a healthy life, all of it wholly consistent with the ideals of Islam. Bilali's book was titled *First Fruits of Happiness* (after translation), it was also known as a "Slave Diary."

Bilali started one of the first Muslim communities in America. While still in slavery, the community built villages similar to those used in Africa. Bilali had 12 sons and 7 daughters. No one seems to know what happened to his sons. He gave Muslim names and traditions to his nineteen children. His daughters' names were Margaret, Hester, Charlotte, Fatima, Yoruba, Medina, and Binty. It is reported that all but Binty could speak English, French, Fulfulde, and Arabic.

Bilali was the slave of a prominent Georgian master named, Thomas Spalding, who often wrote for newspapers. Bilali was the sole manager of the plantation and was directly in charge of more than five hundred of his fellow slaves. Bilali is well-known for twice saving the local community. Once in the War of 1812, when Bilali warned the British that he and his men would defend the Island with their lives and property. Bilali told his master,

27

"I will answer for every Negro of the true faith, but not for the Christians you own." The second time was in 1824, when Bilali saved them from a great hurricane that hit Sapelo Island. He directed them into the cotton and sugar houses that they had made of tabby, from the skills they learned in Africa. Remains of some of these houses are still visible today.

Bilali was known for regularly wearing his fez (Kofi) and a long coat, praying the obligatory prayers facing the east, having his own prayer rug, and always observing the Muslim fast (Ramadan) and two holidays (the two 'ids) when they came. Bilali was buried with his Qur'an and prayer rug.

Pages 10 and 11 of Bilali's Arabic-American manuscript. Photo taken from the Georgia State Library, Atlanta.

Tabby houses on Sapelo Island in Georgia built by Bilali and his community*

Picture by Amir Muhammad, 1997.

---

* Tabby is a mixture of water, lime, sand and sea shells in equal parts.

29

Picture by Amir Muhammad, 1997

Picture by Amir Muhammad, 1997

Built in the early 1800s, the tabby ruin was once a one and a half story, 10 room hospital for the slaves of Retreat, Georgia, on St. Simon Island, which was under Salih Bilali's control. Photo by Amir Muhammad, 1997.

Muslim tombstones found on the Georgia coast

The tombstone of Sambo Swift from the Butler Plantation of Darien, Georgia. Sambo lived from 1811 to 1884. His grave site shows the sign of Muslim belief in the oneness of God. Also, his grave site is facing North-east. Photo by Amir Muhammad, 1997.

George Johnson died in 1964 and was buried in Brunswick, Georgia. His gravestone shows the hand indicating oneness. Photo by Amir Muhammad, 1997.

Sarah Coffee (1844–1914) was buried on the same Butler Plantation as Sambo Swift. Photo by Amir Muhammad, 1997

Steve N. Wills lived from 1887 to 1912. His grave is one of many Muslim graves in Behavior Cemetery on Sapelo Island, Georgia, which face East and have this star on their tombstones. Omar ibn Sayyid also puts this same 5-pointed star in some of his writings (see photo on page 29). Photo by A. Muhammad, 1997.

32

Muslim grave sites found in Arlington Cemetary, Arlington, Virginia.

Ishmael Hall died in 1864, having fought in the Civil War, in the United States Colored Troops. Photo by Amir Muhammad, 1997.

Joseph Solomon was buried in Arlington Cemetary as a civilian because he was among the former slaves living in Freetown (a town created late in the 1860s for former slaves) after slavery. Photo by Amir Muhammad, 1997.

Soloman was also buried in Arlington Cemetary as a civilian because he was a resident of Freetown. Photo by Amir Muhammad, 1997.

Sample Writings of Job and Abdul Rahaman

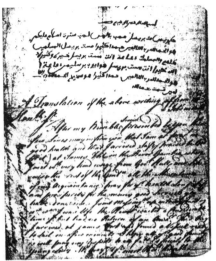

A sample of Abdul Rahaman's Arabic writing.

Job's letter to Nathaniel Brassey, 1734. Courtesy of the British Library and Sidney Kaplan.

A sample of Abdul Rahaman's English writing: an outline of his life.

Samples of Omar ibn (Said) Sayyid's writings

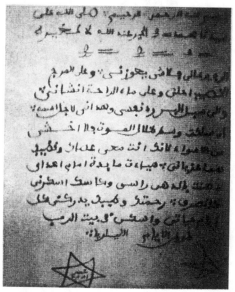

Omar's writing found at Davidson College,
Davidson, NC. Photo by Amir Muhammad.

Some verses from the Qur'an. Photo found in *Africa Remembered*.

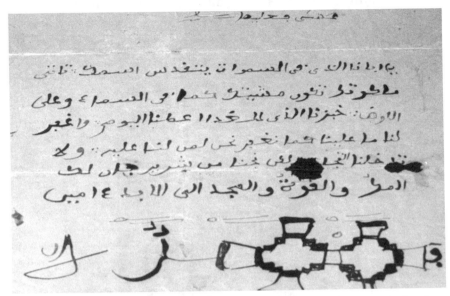

Omar's writing of the Psalms found at Davidson College, Davidson, North Carolina.

The Bible given to Omar in an attempt to convert him to Christianity. Photo by Amir Muhammad.

Abraham, an African American Slave of Chief Micanopy.

Abraham among the Indians. He is behind the others in the middle of the picture.

Picture from Massachusetts
Historical Society, Boston

Muhammad Ali ben Said

Muhammad Ali ben Said known as (Nicholas Said) was born in 1833. He was taken from the heart of Africa by Tuareg bandits around 1849. His family was prominent and he claimed to be the son of Barca Gana, a Bornuese or Bornawa Kashella (General) from Bornoo near Lake Chad. He had served three masters throughout Libya, Turkey, Europe, and parts of Asia.

Muhammad's last slave master Trubetzkoy, a Russian, eventually freed him after some years of service. After Said was freed he worked as a traveler's companion. He made his way to the Caribbean and to South and then North America.

In 1860, Said was offered a chance to return to Africa. Instead, he decided to go to the United States. Unlike most African Americans, Muhammad came to America as a free man. He made his way to Detroit where he worked as a teacher.

When the Civil War broke out, Said joined the 55th Regiment of Massachusetts Colored Volunteers Infantry, Company 1 of the Union Arm. By July 16, 1863, Muhammad had risen from corporal to sergeant. On September 1, 1864, he was reduced from sergeant (at his own request) and detailed to a hospital to acquire some medical knowledge. By 1865, he was honorably discharged.

Muhammad knew nine languages: Arabic, Kanouri, Mandara, Turkish, Russian, English, French, German, and Italian.

Said's autobiography was published in *The Atlantic* under the title "Native of Bornoo." His army records show that he was married and died in Brownsville, Tennessee, in 1882.

Historical Moments

In 1828, a Muslim named Sterling living in Hartford, Connecticut, met Abdul Rahaman during his visit to New England.

In 1830, Charno, a Georgian slave, was asked to show his ability to write. He did so by writing nine lines of a script. He wrote out the *Fatiha* (the first chapter of the Qur'an). He had learned to read and write Arabic in Africa before his capture. Charno was one of the few slaves who left behind a manuscript. Prior to the Civil War, Charno's literary skill was noticed and quoted on a page of Williams A. Caruthers' (1834) novel *The Kentuckian,* published in New York.

In 1834, in Tennessee, a Muslim by the name of Hamet Abdul is reported to have sought money to return to Africa.

In 1834, two Muslims by the names of Jupiter Dowda and Big Jack were reported by the American Colonization Society's *The African Repository* to be well-known slaves in New Orleans. Big Jack was a plantation overseer.

In 1839, Omans' ruler, Sayyid Sa'id, ordered his ship "The Sultana" to set sail for America on a trade mission. The ship touched port in New York on April 30, 1840. The voyage was not a commercial success, but it did mark the beginning of friendly relations between the two countries that has continued until today. The ship's commander, Ahmad Bin Naaman, was reported to have exuded dignity and intelligence. To the surprise of the port officials, he spoke English well. Ahmad Bin Naaman's portrait hangs in the City Hall of New York city.

In 1856, the United States cavalry hired a Muslim by the name of Hajji Ali to experiment with raising camels in Arizona. He became a local folk hero in Quartzsite, Arizona, where he died in 1903.

In 1859 in Savannah, Georgia, many slaves were sold from the Butler plantation, some of them being Muslim. It is recorded that some of the women wore gorgeous turbans and one of them had a string of beads. At the slave auction a Muslim named Abel, age 19, sold for $1,295, and Hagar, age 50, sold for $300. A Muslim named Mingo had a wife and 3 children; the oldest son, Dembo, and his wife were sold for $1,320 to a cotton plantation in Alabama.

In 1860, a Muslim Lady, known as "Old Lizzy Gray," died in Edgefield County. Her obituary, which appeared on the front page of the *Edgefield Advertiser* on September 12th written by her physician and owner, said she was 127 years old and had four children in Africa. In Africa she was reared and educated as a Muslim. She was known in America to have combined the the faiths of Islam and Christianity.

In 1864, Captain Harry Dean was born. He was the son of Susan Cuffe Dean, whose brother was Paul Cuffe. Captain Dean's family came from Quata, Morocco. For three generations the family were wealthy merchants in Philadelphia. Captain Dean founded the first black nautical training school in America. Dean had maintained his family's Islamic tradition during his seafaring days on the ship "Pedro Gorino" and in southern Africa where he tried to build an African empire. He was also associated with the Muslim Mosque of London. In the United States he distributed Islamic literature in Chicago, Los Angeles, Seattle, and Washington State.

In 1866, the last Cherokee chief who had a Muslim name, Ramadan ibn Wati was reported. Muslims were also known to live among the Indians. Many of the Seminole Indians, who lived in Florida and in parts of the swamp lands of Georgia, were runaways and African Muslim slaves. One of the better known Seminole Muslims was Abraham, a slave of Chief Micanopy. Between 1838 and 1843 Abraham traveled as an interpreter with a group of Seminole Chiefs to inspect the land west of the Mississippi River where the U.S. government wanted the Native Americans to move to.

In 1869, a number of Muslims from Yemen arrived in the United States after the opening of the Suez Canal.

By the late 1860s Samba Geladio Jegi became well known as the Sambo of the American folk tales. In West Africa, Samba (Sambo) means second son.

In 1875, the first small wave of Muslim immigrants arrived, mainly from Greater Syria (Syria, Lebanon, and Palestine). A smaller number came from the Punjab of the India subcontinent. Most were unskilled laborers.

In 1883, Sambo Swift died. Born in 1811, he had lived as a slave in Darien, Georgia. He was buried as a Muslim with his grave facing northeast toward Makkah. Engraved on his tombstone is a hand with one finger pointing upward, which is a Muslim symbol representing the one-ness of God. It is believed that Sambo was one of the slaves left on the Butler plantation at the time of the great slave sale of 1859 in Georgia. Sambo was a carpenter and had at least three children—Abraham, Mollie and Alonzo.

In 1889, Edward W. Blyden, a noted scholar and social activist, traveled throughout the eastern and southern parts of the United States proclaiming the truth of Islam.

In 1893, Muhammad Alexander Russell Webb (1846–1916) was the first known white American convert to Islam. Muhammad Webb appeared at the First World Congress of Religions and delivered two lectures: "The Spirit of Islam," and "The Influence of Islam on Social Conditions." Webb converted to Islam in 1888. By trade he was a journalist, and later, a diplomat. In 1897,

42

Webb was appointed by President Cleveland to be an American consul to the Philippines. Webb was an activist for Islam in America; he even founded a Mosque in Manhattan, NY.

In 1898, on October 7, Elijah Muhammad (1898–1975) was born in Sandersville, Georgia. He was the leader of the Nation of Islam from 1934 to 1975. Mr. Muhammad became a force among poor blacks and prisoners before becoming a catalyst for contemporary black political and religious thought. In 1954, he opened the first Islamic School in America called the "University of Islam" in Chicago. By 1954 he had more than 50,000 followers. He is well known for his business success and his "Do for Self" concept of life and work. In December 1959, Mr. Muhammad made the pilgrimage to Mecca.

The 1900s

Historical Moments

In 1900, in Ross, North Dakota, a Muslim group organized to perform the Jumu'ah prayer. It is the earliest known record of such a gathering in North America.

In 1908, there was another wave of Muslim immigrants. Coming to America primarily from the Arab provinces of the Ottoman Empire, Syria, Lebanon, and Jordan, they were mainly Turks, Kurds, Albanians, and Arabs.

In 1913, Noble Drew Ali, at the age of 27, founded the Moorish Science Temple of America in Newark, New Jersey. Ali was born Timothy Drew in January 1886, in Sampson, North Carolina. Drew Ali was commissioned by the Sultan of Morocco to teach Islam to African Americans in the United States. He blended together elements of Islam, black nationalism, and Free-masonry. Noble Drew Ali died in Chicago in 1929. He was given the name Ali by Sultan Abdul Aziz ibn Saud of Mecca.

In 1915, Albanian Muslims opened a mosque in Maine and established an Islamic association. By 1919, they had established another mosque in Connecticut.

Between 1919 and 1922, Islamic associations were formed in Highland Park, Michigan (1919); Detroit, Michigan; and Brooklyn, NY (1922).

In 1921, Dr. Mufti Muhammad Sadiq arrived in the United States and settled in Chicago. He published the first English language Muslim newspaper called *Muslim Sunrise,* of the Ahmadiyya Movement. Some of the Ahmadiyya's Islamic influence was passed on to Noble Drew Ali and Elijah Muhammad. The Ahmadiyyas had an impact on Marcus Garvey's movement, the Moorish Science Temple, and on the Nation of Islam. The Ahmadiyyan community published the first English translation of the Qur'an for use in America in 1917.

In 1922, in Detroit, Michigan, it is believed the first mosque in the United States was built.

In 1926, Duse Muhammad Ali, mentor of Marcus Garvey, helped establish an organization in Detroit known as the Universal Islamic Society. Its motto was "One God, One Aim, One Destiny." He was also known to be frequently in the company of Muhammad Pickthall, the English Muslim scholar who translated the Holy Qur'an into English. Duse had considerable influence upon Garvey's movement.

In 1926, Polish-speaking Tatars opened a mosque in Brooklyn, New York, which is still in use today.

In 1928, the Islamic Propagation Center of America opened on State Street in Brooklyn, New York, under the leadership of Shaykh al-Haj Daoud Ahmed Faisal. He also started the Islamic Mission Society which was active from 1934 to 1942. Shaykh Faisal was granted a charter by Shaykh Khalid of Jordan and King Saud of Saudi Arabia to propagate Islam in America.

In 1930, the Nation of Islam (NOI) was founded. It was one of the most significant organizations in the African-American Muslim community and in African-American history. It was responsible for converting a large number of African Americans to Islam, and it was effective in highlighting the effects of slavery and racism. The NOI's philosophy was introduced into the United States by Fard Muhammad (Wallace D. Fard), who disappeared in 1934. Elijah Mohammed, who succeeded Fard in 1934, built the organization into a strong ethnic movement.

The movement produced many upright and successful Muslims, and at least four famous African-American Muslims, El-Haj Malik al-Shabazz (Malcolm X), Muhammad Ali, Warith D. Mohammed, and Louis Farrakhan. All of them, with the exception of Mr. Farrakhan, embraced orthodox Islam.

Influenced by the Nation of Islam, the spelling of Arabic words already in use in the English language were changed to correctly represent their Arabic pronunciation. For example, "Moslem" was changed to "Muslim," "Mahomet" to "Muhammad," and "Koran" to "Qur'an."

In the 1930s, mosques were started in Dearborn, Michigan; Michigan City, Michigan; Sacramento, California; Pennsylvania; and Cleveland, Ohio.

In 1930, the Georgia Writers Project (a Works Progress Administration program), which collected stories of living ex-slaves, documented 18 ex-slaves who were Muslims. Some of their names were recalled by their descendants in 1930. The women that were remembered were Phoebe (who was Bilali Muhammad's wife),

Hannah, Ryna, Patience Spalding, and Rachel Grant. There were two men remembered, their names were given as Calina and Old Israel.

In 1934, the Lebanese community of Cedar Rapids, Iowa, opened the first building specifically built to be a mosque in America, under the leadership of Abdullah Ingram.

In 1945, African-American Muslims purchased a building and established the first mosque in Pittsburgh, Pennsylvania. This was the first mosque to be chartered by indigenous Muslims in the USA.

In 1946, the first Young Muslim Women's Association was chartered in Pittsburgh, Pennsylvania. They had a sub-charter in Missouri that provided services such as aid for dependent children, widows, and the elderly.

Between 1947 and 60, the third wave of Muslim immigrants came to the United States from Palestine, Yugoslavia, Lebanon, and Egypt.

In 1952, Muslims in the military sued the federal government and were allowed to identify themselves as Muslims.

In 1956, Malcolm X became an active preacher for the Nation of Islam. He started working with the Nation of Islam in 1952 when he was released from jail.

In 1957, the Islamic Center of Washington, D.C., opened.

In 1958, the Hanafi Madh-Hab Center was organized by Hammas Abdul Khaalis in Washington, D.C. He was a former member and official of the Nation of Islam. The basketball player, Kareem Abdul-Jabbar later became a prominent member of the organization.

In 1960, the first African-American Muslim newspaper, *Muhammad Speaks,* was launched. It became the largest minority weekly paper in the country. At its peak it reached more than 800,000 readers. Since its conception it has undergone various name changes. It became the *Bilalian News* the *The American Muslim Journal.* Currently its name is *The Muslim Journal.*

In the 1960s, the largest Sunni Muslim community of African Americans was centered in Brooklyn, New York. Shaykh Daoud and Malcolm X had their mosques in Brooklyn, New York.

Between 1960 and 1980, a fourth wave of Muslim students and immigrants came to America from all over the Muslim world.

In 1962, Darul-Islam started under the leadership of Imam Yahya Abdul Karim, Ishaq A. Shaheed, and Rajab Mahmu in Brooklyn, New York. In the 1980s the community came under the influence of Shaykh Jaylani. Many in the community rejected his teachings and eventually pledged allegiance to Imam Jamil Al-Amin.

In 1963, the Muslim Student's Association (MSA) was founded. It assists foreign Muslim students attending schools in the United States. The MSA now has more than 100 branches nationwide.

In 1964, Clarence 13X founded the Five Percenters after leaving the Nation of Islam in New York. Many rap groups and singers identify with the Five Percenters. Clarence 13x was killed in 1969.

In 1965, Internationally known Muslim leader Malcolm X (El-Haj Malik al-Shabazz) was assassinated in New York.

In 1967, the Ansaru Allah community was organized in New York.

As-Sayyid Isa Al Haadi Al Mahdi was the founder of the organization, which changed its name a few times. First it was Ansar Pure Sufi, then Nubian Islamic Hebrews. Isa was born in 1945 in Omdurman, Sudan. Shaykh Daoud was one of Isa's mentors.

From 1970 to 1973 Dr. Fazlur Rahman Khan, a Muslim from Bangladesh, designed Chicago's John Hancock Center (1970), the One Shell Plaza in Houston (1971), and the Sears Towers in Chicago (1973).

In 1974, The Muslim World League was granted non-governmental organization status at the United Nations.

In 1975, February 25, Elijah Muhammad, leader of the Nation of Islam, died.

In 1975, Warith Deen Mohammed (born in 1933), became the leader of the Nation of Islam. He moved the Nation of Islam from black nationalism to the universal religion of Islam, and in 1985 he decentralized the community. Under his leadership the community experienced many positive transitions and made the following name changes: The World Community of Al-Islam in the West (1976–1981); The American Muslim Mission (1981–1985); The Ministry of W.D. Mohammed (1985–1997); and most recently, The Muslim American Society (1997). Mr. Muhammad is known as the Muslim American Spokesman for Human Salvation. He is credited with influencing the African American leadership to call themselves African Americans, instead of what they had been calling themselves, Black Americans.

In 1978, Warith Deen Muhammad was named consultant and trustee by the Gulf States to distribute funds for Islamic missionary activities in the U.S.

In 1981, the first Islamic library was established in Plainfield, Indiana.

In 1982, the Islamic Society of North America (ISNA) was established as an umbrella organization seeking to meet the needs of both transient students and resident American Muslims. It is headquartered in Plainfield, Indiana.

In 1985, the Muslim League of Voters (MLV) was established in Irvington, New Jersey. The MLV was established to promote political and economic dignity.

In 1990, the American Muslim Council (AMC) was established in Washington, D.C. The AMC is one of the leading Muslim political organizations in the United States serving the Muslim community.

In 1991, Imam Siraj Wahhaj became the first Muslim in U.S. history to recite the invocation (opening prayer) in the United States House of Representatives.

In 1992, Imam Warith Deen Mohammed became the first Muslim in U.S. history to offer the invocation (opening prayer) in the United States Senate.

In 1993, Captain Abdul Rasheed became the first Muslim Army Chaplin (Imam) in the U.S. Army.

In 1996, LTJG Monje Malak Noel became the first Muslim Naval Chaplin (Imam) in the U.S. Navy.

In 1996, the AMC sponsored the first *iftar* (the meal breaking the daily fast during Ramadan) on Capitol Hill. The White House and First Lady Hillary Rodham Clinton, recognized the completion of Ramadan by hosting a group of Muslim families at a White House reception for *'id al-fitr* (the celebration ending the fast of Ramadan) sponsored by the AMC.

Throughout the 80s and 90s the Muslim community in the United States has seen much growth. Today, Islam is the fastest growing religion in America and is rapidly becoming its second largest religion. Across the country, there are many Muslims who hold elected offices as state representatives, mayors, and judges. Many also work for state and local governments. Today, we find Muslims in every profession.

In 1997, more than 1,000 documented mosques and Islamic centers are found in the United States where an estimated 6 to 8 million Muslims live. There are five cities with more than 20 mosques and Islamic centers: Houston, Texas (31); Brooklyn, New York (25); Detroit, Michigan (24); Chicago, Illinois (24); and Philadelphia, Pennsylvania (20).

Contributions and Personalities

In Sports

Muhammad Ali is one of the most famous and recognized Muslim personalities in the world this century. A three-time World Heavyweight Boxing Champion, he is well known as the people's champion and as a strong Muslim. Other boxers who were Muslims during their careers are Saad Muhammad, Eddie Mustafa, Dwight Braxten (Muhammad Qawi-Ali), and now Mike Tyson.

Kareem Abdul-Jabbar, was a basketball Hall-of-Famer who played for the LA Lakers. Other famous Muslim basketball players were Jamal Wilkes, of the LA Lakers; Walt Hazzard, of the Atlanta Hawks; Charlie Scott (Shaheed Abdul-Aleem), and Spencer Haywood, of the Phoenix Suns. Today, the great Muslim basketball players are Hakeem Olajuwon, of the Houston Rockets; Mahmoud Abdul-Rauf, of the Denver Nuggets; AbdurRahim, of Vancouver; and Craig Hodges.

Ahmad Rashad, former football receiver for the Minnesota Vikings, now a national sportscaster; Abdus-Salaam, former tackle for the New York Jets; Raghib (Rocket) Ismail, receiver for the LA Raiders; Salaam, running back for the Chicago Bears; and Abdul Jabbar, of the Miami Dolphins are a few of the many outstanding Muslim football players. There are also many outstanding College Muslim athletes.

In Art and Entertainment

In the field of jazz, there are many Muslim entertainers; examples include jazz great McCoy Tyner (Sulaiman Saud), Pharaoh Sanders, Ahmad Jamal, Art Blakely, Yusef Lateef, Talib Daud, Idris Muhammad, Najee, Rahsaan Roland Kirk, Jamal Nasser, Nasser Abberde', Talib Kibwaye, Ahmed Abdul-Malik, Sabu Adeyola, and South African born Abdullah Ibrahim.

R&B song writer and producer Muhammad Luqman Abdul-Haqq (Kenny Gamble) of the writing team Gamble and Huff was responsible for the Philadelphia Sound of the late 1960s through the early 1980s. Many famous songs performed by the Philadelphia recording artists had an Islamic influence in them like, "Give the People What They Want," "Together," "Love Train," "Unity," "Family Reunion," "Survival," "You Can't Hide from Yourself," and "Message in Our Music."

Many of the popular singers are Muslims, such as Khalis Bayyan (Ronald Bell), Amir Abdul-Salaam Bayyan (Kevin Bell), and Muhammad (Kool) Bayyan from the music group *Kool and the Gang*. In addition, there is Abdul-Aziz (Joe Tex); Abdul Fakir, a member of the *Four Tops*, a Motown Hall of Fame group; Talib Muhammad (Ted Miller), the former lead singer of *Blue Magic*; William Hart of the *Delfonics*; Mark Greene, the original lead singer of the *Moments*; the Motown group, *The Boys*; and Wyclef of the group *Fugees*.

Islam has influenced rap music from the beginning with *The Last Poets* known as the original rap group.

Currently, there are Muslim members in the groups *Tribe, Groove Theory, Ever Last, Public Enemy;* and there are other rappers like Q-Tip and Lakim Shabazz to name only a few. There is also reggae star Jimmy Cliff, and pop star Yusuf Islam (Cat Stevens).

Many Muslims are producers and executives in the music and entertainment business like Abdul Jalil of Super Star Management, Qasim Ahmed of Creative Entertainment, and Royal Bayyan, a record executive, to name only a few.

There are Muslim actors, writers, and producers like Moustapha Akkad, the producer of *The Message, Lion of the Desert, The Story of Islam,* and the blockbuster hit *Halloween.*

Actor, Luqman (Roger) of the early 70s T.V. show *What's Happening.*

Actor, Omar Epps comes from a Muslim family, as does world renown model and actress Imani.

Askia Muhammad Toure (Rolland Snelling) is well known as a poet and played a very important role in the development of Black Arts in the 1960s and 1970s.

Imamu Amiri Baraka (Leroy Jones) was a prominent poet and activist in the 1960s and 1970s. He has many books to his credit.

Eugene Majeed is a well-known Muslim illustrator whose work reflects the spiritual and metaphysical wisdom of the African-American Muslim community in the early 1970s.

Mohamed Zakariya is credited as being the person who started the art of Islamic calligraphy in the United States. His work is exhibited and sold throughout the world. Zakariya is the first American to receive a diploma from the Research Center for Islamic History, Art, and Culture in Istanbul, Turkey.

In the Social Field

Nobel Drew Ali was the leader of the Moorish Science Temples from 1913 to 1929. The Honorable Elijah Muhammad was the leader of the Nation of Islam from 1934 to 1975. Malcolm X (El-Hajj Malik El-Shabazz) was a strong Muslim and Human rights leader from 1956 to 1965. These men were great leaders and influenced hundreds of thousands Muslims and non-Muslims. They helped reform and educate many poor and unlettered people. The impact of their leadership is felt even today.

Imam Warith Deen Mohammed is the current leader of the largest indigenous Muslim community in America. His leadership has grown worldwide. Many members of this community are known as Muslim Americans and Bilalians, to reflect their Islamic and African cultural heritage.

Other renowned leaders are Jamil Al-Amin (H. Rap Brown), Siraj Wahhaj, Dr. Naim Akbar, Dr. Khalid Abdullah Tarik Al-Mansur, and the Nation of Islam (NOI) leader, Louis Farrakhan.

Betty Shabazz, wife of Malcolm X, was a woman of exemplary courage, compassion, and dignity. She has been and continues to be an inspiration to many. Shabazz was a mother, educator, college administrator, child advocate, civil rights leader, widow, and keeper of Malcolm X's legacy.

Bogdan Ataullah Kopanski, a Polish-American with a Ph.D. in history and politics embraced Islam in 1974.

Maryam Jameelah (Margaret Marcus) was born into a Jewish family and converted to Islam. She is best known as an essayist, journalist, and author of many books.

Alim Fatah was instrumental in the development of the self-adhesive U.S. Postage Stamp in use today.

In Politics

The first recorded Muslim political activity was in 1753 when Abel Conder and Mahamut won their freedom after they petitioned the South Carolina House of Representatives.

In 1991, Charles Bilal of Kountze, Texas, became the nation's first Muslim Mayor.

There are many elected Muslim officials around the country. To name a few there is Yusuf Abdus-Salaam, a city councilman in Selma, Alabama; the first elected Muslim woman, Lateefah Muhammad, is a city councilwoman in Tuskegee, Alabama; Yusuf Abdul-Hakeem is city councilman and president in Chattanooga,

Tennessee; Nasif Rashad Majeed is a city councilman in Charlotte, North Carolina; Larry Shaw is a state senator in North Carolina; Bilal Beasley is a city councilman and president in Irvington, New Jersey; Jimmy Small Salaam is a councilman in East Orange, New Jersey; Oscar Brooks is a councilman in Pemberton Township, New Lisbon, New Jersey; John Rhodes is a councilman, in North Las Vegas, Nevada; Natalie Bayton, is a council-woman in Oakland, California; Benjamine Ahmad is a councilman in Menlo, California; and Suzanne Sareni is a councilwoman in Dearborn, Michigan.

All around the country there are Muslims who are appointed officials. In the near future, two of the current councilmen intend to run for mayor in their cities—Nasif Majeed, in North Carolina, and Bilal Beasley, in New Jersey.

Reference Material

Haddad, Yvonne Y. "A Century of Islam in America." In *Islamic Affairs Programs*. 1986.

Curtin, Philip. *Africa Remembered: Narratives by West Africans from the Slave Trade*. Madison, WI, 1968.

McCloud, Aminah Beverly. *African American Islam*. Routledge, NJ, 1995.

Austin, Allan. *African Muslims in Antebellum America: A Source Book*. New York, 1984.

Ferris, Marc. *American Legacy; America's First Black Muslims*. 1997.

Hagy, James. "Muslims Slaves." *Carologue* (South Carolina Historical Society) Spring, 1993.

Windley, Lathan. *Georgia and Maryland Runaway Slaves Advertisements,* n.d.

Koszegi, M. and J. Gordon Melton. *Islam in North America (A Source book)*. Garland Publishing, 1992.

Rashad, Adib. *Islam, Black Nationalism & Slavery (A Detailed History)*. Beltsville, MD: Printers, Inc., 1995.

Numan, Fareed. *The Muslim Population in the United States*. Washington, DC: The American Muslim Council, 1992.

Abdul-Khaliq, Salim. *The Untold Story of Blacks in Islam*. U.B. & U.S. Communications Systems, 1994.

Brandon Institute. *Muslims in Georgia: A Chronology & Oral History.* 1993.

What Became of the Slaves on a Georgia Plantation: A sequel to Mrs. Kemble's Journal. 1863.